# WHY DO EARTHQUAKES HAPPEN?

WIL MARA

 **Marshall Cavendish**
Benchmark
New York

Other Marshall Cavendish Offices:
Marshall Cavendish International (Asia) Private Limited, 1 New Industrial Road, Singapore 536196 • Marshall Cavendish International (Thailand) Co Ltd. 253 Asoke, 12th Flr, Sukhumvit 21 Road, Klongtoey Nua, Wattana, Bangkok 10110, Thailand • Marshall Cavendish (Malaysia) Sdn Bhd, Times Subang, Lot 46, Subang Hi-Tech Industrial Park, Batu Tiga, 40000 Shah Alam, Selangor Darul Ehsan, Malaysia

Marshall Cavendish is a trademark of Times Publishing Limited

All websites were available and accurate when this book was sent to press.

Library of Congress Cataloging-in-Publication Data
Mara, Wil.
  How do earthquakes happen? / by Wil Mara.
    p. cm. — (Tell me why, tell me how)
  Includes index.
  Summary: "Provides comprehensive information on the process of earthquakes forming"—Provided by publisher.
  ISBN 978-0-7614-4826-6
  1. Earthquakes—Juvenile literature. I. Title.
  QE521.3.M28 2011
  551.22—dc22
2009033494

Photo research by Candlepants Incorporated

Cover Photo: Code Red / Getty Images

The photographs in this book are used by permission and through the courtesy of:
*Getty Images*: Sam Yeh/AFP, 1; Andy Ryan, 5; Andy Crawford, 8; D'Arco Editori, 12; Jon Van de Grift/Visuals Unlimited, Inc., 13; Andrew Green, 14; Dennis Lane Photography, 15; Baron Wolman, 16; WIN-Initiative, 18; James Stevenson, 22. *Alamy Images*: Garry Gay, 4; Guy Croft SciTech, 23; Edward Parker, 24; Arctic Imades, 19. *Photo Researchers Inc.*: Gary Hincks, 6, 9; Daniel Sambraus, 7; SPL, 10; David A. Hardy, 20.

Editor: Joy Bean
Publisher: Michelle Bisson
Art Director: Anahid Hamparian
Series Designer: Alex Ferrari

Printed in Malaysia (T)
135642

# CONTENTS

A powerful earthquake can easily destroy homes and other buildings.

# Big Plates

Imagine that you are walking down the street. The ground beneath your feet suddenly begins to shake. It shakes hard enough to make you lose your balance and fall down. Now imagine the ground shaking so hard that the buildings around you begin to crumble. Chunks of concrete hit the ground. Telephone poles tip over. Cars are tossed around like toys. Then the street cracks in half. Underground pipes explode, and plumes of water and gas shoot into the air. Sounds scary, right? This is an earthquake.

It is easy to think of Earth as a solid ball, but it is not solid. One of the

An earthquake caused this road to split.

reasons earthquakes happen is that the outer shell of Earth is broken up into separate sections called **tectonic plates**. Think of it like a scoop of vanilla ice cream with one of those delicious chocolate shells on the outside. If you put your hand over the shell and squeezed gently, the shell would begin to crack in many places. Each of the pieces is like a tectonic plate.

The lines where tectonic plates meet are called **plate boundaries**. Let us use our ice cream comparison again. You would see white lines of vanilla ice cream between the cracked parts of chocolate shell. These white lines are like plate boundaries.

There are eight main tectonic plates

The boundaries of Earth's tectonic plates are seen here in red.

on Earth, plus many smaller ones. Each plate is huge. For example, the land that makes up Canada, the United States, and Mexico is part of just one plate. It is called the North American plate.

This valley walkway in Iceland is the boundary between the North American and the European tectonic plates.

The earth is made up of
many different layers.

# Moving Plates

Believe it or not, giant tectonic plates actually move. Even though they are made up of very hard material, they sit on different material that is hot and rubbery.

If you cut Earth in half, you would see that it is made up of several layers. In the middle you would see a circle. This is Earth's **core**. The core is surrounded by a series of rings, each larger than the one before it. The rings represent the rest of Earth's layers.

Tectonic plates are made up of the top two layers—the Earth's **crust** and the upper parts of the **mantle**. These layers

Even though they are huge, tectonic plates move. This illustration shows the direction of their movement.

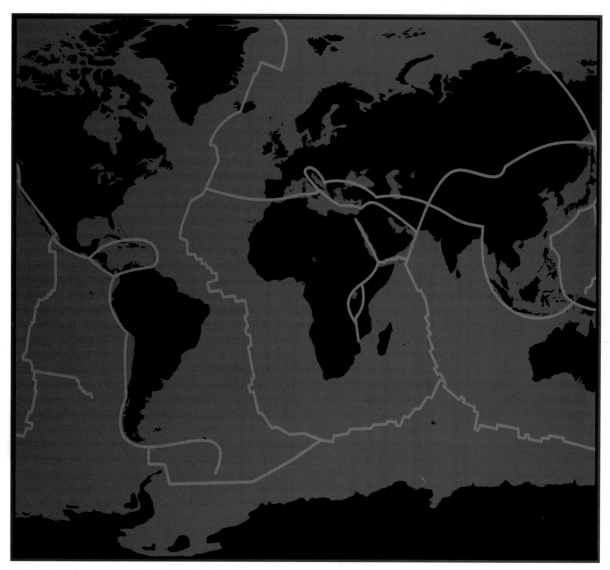

Tectonic plates vary in size and shape.

are very hard and rocky.
But the layers right beneath
them are so hot that they
are almost like a very thick
liquid. These layers are the
lower parts of the mantle and

the upper parts of the core. This means tectonic plates drift
in a kind of enormous pool of hot liquid. Think about our ice
cream cone again. When the ice cream starts to melt, the
pieces of the chocolate shell can move around very easily.
This is similar to what happens with tectonic plates.

Tectonic plates do not move very far. In one year, they
shift only about 2 to 4 inches (50 to 100 millimeters). It may
not sound like much, but this is enough movement to get an
earthquake started.

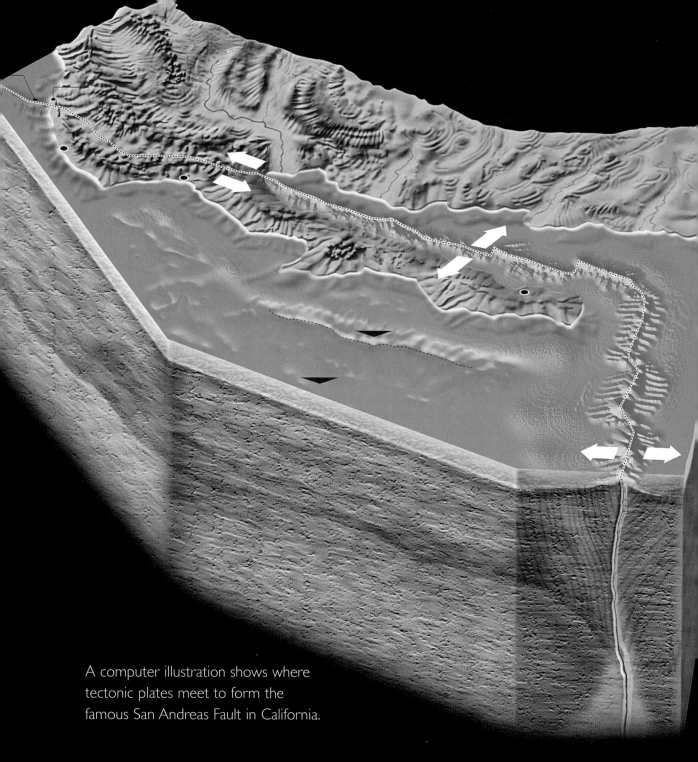

A computer illustration shows where tectonic plates meet to form the famous San Andreas Fault in California.

# Stressing Out

Sometimes as tectonic plates move around the earth, they will bump against each other. As a result, they might get stuck together. When this happens, it puts an enormous amount of stress on the land near the boundaries. The plates stay stuck together, but the land around them keeps trying to move. If the plates stick too long, the stress builds and builds. If a nearby area of Earth's crust and upper mantle is weak, the land begins to crack. This can start either many miles below the surface or very close to the surface.

An earthquake caused the damage in this field in Hawaii.

If the land cracks quickly and violently, an earthquake starts deep within the earth. Usually this crack occurs deep underground, so you would not be able to feel it. The spot where the crack starts is called the earthquake's **focus**. The spot on the ground right above the focus is called the earthquake's **epicenter**. Most of the time, the focus is less than 45 miles (72 kilometers) below the ground. Sometimes,

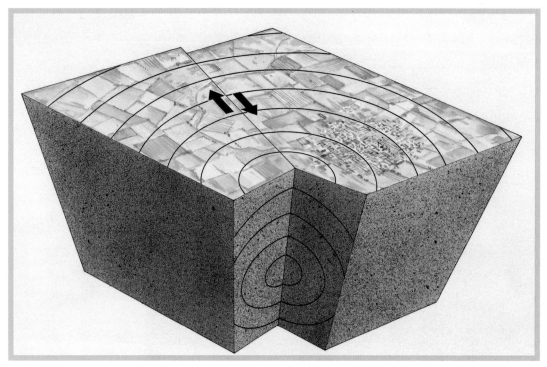

Seismic waves move upward from their focus until they reach the Earth's surface. That point is then called the earthquake's epicenter.

however, the focus can be more than 400 miles (645 km) below the earth's surface.

When the land breaks apart violently, a tremendous amount of energy is produced. This energy travels through the ground in the form of **seismic waves**. These are similar to the waves you see when you drop a toy into a bathtub. Rippling circles grow away from the spot where the toy hits the water. These are energy waves. The only difference

Seismic waves ripple through the earth similar to the way a single drop of water will cause ripples in a pool.

between water waves and seismic waves is that water waves travel through water, while seismic waves go through land. It is no surprise that the word *seismic* comes from the Greek word *seismos*, which means "earthquake."

Seismic waves show themselves when the crack that began the earthquake grows larger. Since the seismic waves travel in every direction (just like the waves in the bathtub), the crack becomes wider.

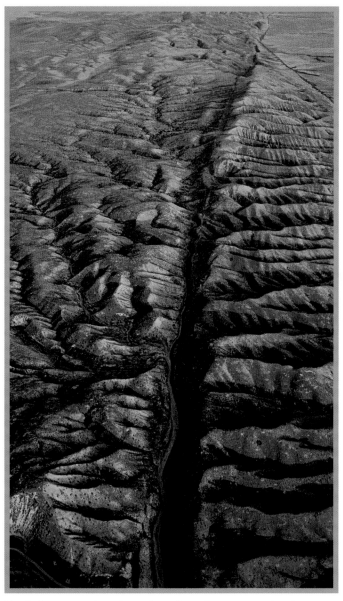

Fault lines can be thought of as deep scars in the earth's surface.

Sometimes it reaches up to the surface of the earth. This is when an earth-quake's **fault line**, or crack in the earth that the earthquake created, appears.

Now I Know!

What is the name of the exact spot where a crack in the earth first appears?

The focus.

The fault can grow amazingly fast—about 2 miles (3 km) per second. If a car traveled that fast, it would be going 720 miles per hour (1,152 kilometers per hour)!

Seismic waves become weaker as they travel farther from the epicenter. That means an earthquake is most powerful—and most destructive—at its epicenter. Eventually, the waves lose power and die out. It may be hard to believe, but small earthquakes occur deep in the ground every day. Most, however, are not strong enough for us to feel. That is because the seismic waves are not that strong. They die out before they reach the surface.

# The Deadly Shake

When seismic waves reach the ground, people can feel an earthquake. There are different types of seismic waves, and each type has a different effect. One type causes the ground—and anything attached to the ground—to stretch. For example, a road might get ripped apart. Another type of wave shakes everything back and forth. This wave type is very dangerous because it can cause heavy things to come flying down. For example, an air conditioner sitting in a high window could

Seismic waves caused this road in Iceland to stretch and break apart.

shake loose and zoom through the air. A third kind of wave rolls through the ground, similar to the up-and-down motion of an ocean wave. These waves can be so powerful that they flip cars and trucks over.

When all these waves occur at the same time, a very deadly earthquake occurs. Buildings collapse, bridges snap, and boulders begin tumbling down the sides of mountains. If a dam breaks, a town can be flooded in a matter of

Tsunamis are often caused by undersea earthquakes. They can destroy entire towns and claim many lives.

minutes. Power lines, brimming with millions of electrical volts, can break free and **electrocute** someone. Gas lines explode, and fires start everywhere. If a powerful earthquake happens deep in the ocean, it can trigger a **tsunami**—a giant swell of water that can wipe out entire towns in a matter of minutes.

An earthquake usually lasts only a minute or so. That is a lot of destruction in such a short span of time! There are also smaller quakes before and after the main one. Those that come before the main earthquake are called **foreshocks**, and those that come afterward are called **aftershocks**.

Now I Know!

What can an earthquake that happens deep in the ocean cause?

A tsunami.

Seismometers are used to measure the strength of an earthquake.

# Listening, Measuring, and Building

Scientists use a machine called a **seismometer** to measure the strength of an earthquake. A seismometer draws lines back and forth on long rolls of paper that are always moving. The stronger the earthquake, the wider the lines are.

This seismometer is recording minor Earth tremors.

We determine an earthquake's strength by observing how much energy it puts out when it strikes. Devices called **sensors** help scientists figure out the power of the shaking. Then they give this power a number value based on something called the **moment magnitude scale**. This scale tells the size of the quake. A very strong earthquake would rate 7.0 or higher on the moment magnitude scale, while a small one might rate around 2.5.

Scientists cannot tell way ahead of time if an earthquake is going to happen. Even sensors near busy earthquake zones detect slight tremors only about a minute or so before a powerful quake hits. The sensors are connected to emergency systems that send out alert messages to nearby towns and cities. People do not have much time to react.

In years past, buildings and bridges often crumbled during strong earthquakes. This has

This building in Mexico City was designed to withstand the shock of a powerful earthquake.

caused the deaths of thousands of people. In recent years, however, architects and **engineers** have become much better at something called

**earthquake-resistant design**. This is a way to make buildings, bridges, and other structures better able to hold up against the force of earthquakes. One way is to use **dampers**, which are like large springs. Dampers allow a building or a bridge to move gently during a quake, and they also absorb much of the earthquake's energy.

Builders also use building material that can flex without breaking easily. Believe it or not, steel and iron are fairly flexible. Something like concrete is more brittle and will crumble rather than bend.

## Activity

### Make a Simple Seismometer

You can make a very basic seismometer with common items in your home.

### What You Will Need

- a small box, such as a shoebox
- a magic marker with a thin tip
- a piece of string
- a roll of tape
- three wooden sticks, such as one from an ice pop

### What to Do

1. Tape two of the wooden sticks together, end to end, so they make one long stick. Then tape the third wooden stick to the end of the other two so it creates an L shape.

2. Have an adult help you make a thin slit in the top of the shoebox. You will put the long wooden sticks through here. You may have to use some

more tape to keep the sticks steady. Once this step is done, it should look like you are ready to play a game of hangman.

3. Tape a piece of string to the end of a magic marker. Tape the other end of the string to the L-shaped end of the wooden stick so that the marker hangs from it. *Make sure the tip of the marker is just barely touching the surface of the shoebox.*

4. Put a piece of blank paper under the tip of the marker. The marker should be able to touch the paper.

5. Shake the box slightly with one hand, and slowly pull the paper away with the other hand. The back-and-forth lines you see are similar to the lines produced by a real seismometer.

6. Now shake the box a little harder. This increases the power of your "earthquake."

#  Glossary

**aftershocks**—Small quakes that happen after a main earthquake.

**core**—The center layer of Earth.

**crust**—The outermost layer of Earth.

**dampers**—Large, springlike devices that allow a structure to move slightly and absorb energy shocks during an earthquake.

**earthquake-resistant design**—A way to construct buildings, bridges, and other structures so they can hold up to the force of an earthquake.

**electrocute**—To kill by electric shock.

**engineers**—A person trained and skilled in the design, construction, and use of engines or machines.

**epicenter**—The spot on Earth's surface directly above an earthquake's focus.

**fault line**—The crack in the earth that an earthquake creates.

**focus**—The spot within Earth where cracking begins prior to an earthquake.

**foreshocks**—Small quakes that happen before a main earthquake.

**mantle**—The second outermost layer of Earth, just below the crust.

**moment magnitude scale**—A system that scientists use to give the power of an earthquake a number value so the quake can be measured and recorded.

**plate boundaries**—Areas between two tectonic plates.

**seismic waves**—Waves of energy that travel through the earth during an earthquake.

**seismometer** (also called a seismograph)—An instrument that measures the strength of an earthquake.

**sensors**—Devices that detect the movements caused by an earthquake.

**tectonic plates**—Large, separate masses of crust and upper mantle that make up the outer surface (the "shell") of Earth.

**tsunami**—A huge swell of water produced by energy waves following an undersea earthquake.

# Find Out More

## BOOKS

Bauer, Marion Dane. *Earthquake!* New York, NY: Aladdin Books, 2009.

Green, Jen. *Understanding Volcanoes and Earthquakes*. New York, NY: PowerKids Press, 2008.

Griffey, Harriet. *Earthquakes and Other Natural Disasters*. New York, NY: DK Readers, 2010.

O'Shei, Tim. *Tornadoes, Earthquakes, and Other Phenomena: The Curious Kid's Guide to Our Powerful Planet*. Montreal, Canada: Lobster Press, 2008.

Riley, Joelle. *Earthquakes*. Minneapolis, MN: Lerner Publications, 2007.

## WEBSITES

Fun and interesting information about earthquakes, including puzzles, games, pictures, and more.
http://earthquake.usgs.gov/learn/kids/

Features animated earthquake-related images, a map of the world's tectonic plates, diagrams of the different types of faults, and much more.
www.weatherwizkids.com/weather-earthquake.htm

Provides links to sites with information on all aspects of earthquakes.
http://sciencespot.net/Pages/kdzethsci2.html

# Index

Page numbers in **boldface** are illustrations.